CONTENTS

How did life change in Victorian times?

Queen Victoria ruled Britain from 1837 until her death in 1901. The people who lived during this period are known as the Victorians. At this time, Britain was one of the most powerful countries in the world, controlling a large empire abroad and leading the world in industry and trade. Victoria's reign also saw the arrival of many great ideas and inventions that helped to shape the modern world.

This photograph of Queen Victoria sitting at a spinning wheel was taken in 1857.

Below, Victorian women work in a cycle factory in Coventry.

'The nineteenth century has seen a whole cycle of changes. The steam engine locomotive by land and sea, steam applied to printing and manufacture, the electric telegraph, photography, cheap newspapers, penny postage, chloroform gas, the electric light, iron ships, revolvers of all sorts, sewing machines, omnibuses and cabs, parcel deliveries, post office savings banks, people's baths, drinking fountains and a thousand minutiae [little details] of life, such as matches.'

A Victorian commentator writing in 1887.

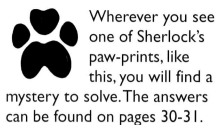
The Victorian age was a time when life in Britain changed more dramatically than ever before. Among the most important changes were the great advances made in manufacturing. Britain in Victorian times became known as the 'workshop of the world' because of the huge quantities of goods that British factories made and sold abroad. There had been some factories in Britain since the eighteenth century but the Victorian period saw a huge increase in their number and size. This was part of what historians call the 'industrial revolution', a process that made Britain very rich and had a dramatic effect on where and how its people lived their lives.

Wherever you see one of Sherlock's paw-prints, like this, you will find a mystery to solve. The answers can be found on pages 30-31.

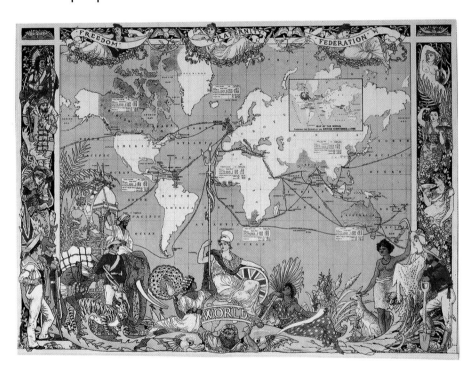

A map of the British Empire in 1886. The countries controlled by Britain are shown in pink.

In this book we are going to investigate Victorian factories and the lives of the people who worked in them. To help with your investigation you will need to look for evidence in order to prepare your own project on Victorian factories. The history detective Sherlock Bones will help you by suggesting where to search for clues. Much of the information that you need is available on the Internet. You will find a list of useful websites at the end of this book.

DETECTIVE WORK

Look in libraries for books about the Victorians. You could also ask your relatives if they have any old photographs taken during the Victorian age, especially those showing working people.

DID EVERYONE LIKE THE FACTORIES?

Women working in a Lancashire cotton mill in 1897.

Waterwheels were used to provide power for early factories.

The first factories were set up in the eighteenth century to produce textiles such as cotton. They were built next to fast-flowing rivers and powered by waterwheels. With the introduction of steam power, factories could be built anywhere that could provide a good supply of coal. As steam engines were more powerful than waterwheels, factory owners could build larger factories with bigger and faster machines.

Before the invention of factories, most of the things that people bought were made by skilled workers in small workshops or their own homes. These goods took a long time to make and were often expensive. Because the machinery in factories could produce goods much faster, more cheaply and in much greater quantities than they could be produced by hand, many independent workers were forced out of business.

'A steam engine with the strength of 880 men can work 50,000 spindles. All this needs only 750 workers, to make as much yarn as 200,000 men did before.'

A Victorian manufacturer

This boy is helping his mother to spin wool.

Spinners and weavers were among the first to be affected. Their hand looms and spinning wheels had no chance of matching the pace of new machines such as John Kay's 'flying shuttle' and James Hargreaves' 'spinning jenny'. These could produce miles of fabric at dazzling speed.

At first, some skilled craftsmen tried to protect their livelihoods by attacking factories and smashing the hated machines. Such protests died out during Victoria's reign as people came to realize that the rapid spread of the factories could not be stopped.

DETECTIVE WORK

Look in libraries for copies of Kelly's Business Directories containing information about factories in your area during Victorian times. Find out what the factories produced, who owned them and how many workers were employed there. You can also get information from the Internet by searching for 'Kelly's Directories'.

These heavily armed people (right) are on their way to smash up a factory. Mobs like this were sometimes called 'Luddites' after one of their leaders – Ned Ludd.

✿ What do you think the rioters in the picture are going to use to destroy the factory?

WHERE DID FACTORY WORKERS LIVE?

'The cellar in which a family of human beings lived was very dark inside. Three or four children were rolling on the damp… wet, brick floor, through which the stagnant, filthy moisture of the street oozed up; the fire-place was empty and black.'

Extract from *Mary Barton*, a novel written in 1848 by Elizabeth Gaskell

Before the arrival of factories, there were few large towns and cities in Britain. Most people lived and worked in the countryside. As more and more factories were built, brand new towns appeared. Existing towns grew much bigger as people poured in from the countryside in search of work.

Many Victorian factory workers lived in slums like those above.

By the end of the nineteenth century, most Victorians lived in towns and cities. But people arriving from the country often had to live in dreadful conditions. Homes in the parts of towns where factory workers lived were often badly built and poorly looked after. In these slum areas, as many houses as possible were packed together around dismal courtyards linked by dark, narrow streets.

Inside the houses, many families cooked, ate, bathed and slept together in single rooms that offered little or no privacy. Water for cleaning and drinking had to be fetched inside from shared wells and pumps. These were often contaminated by sewage or by chemicals from the factories. Rubbish rotted in the courtyards and alleyways, attracting rats.

The cramped and dirty conditions of the towns encouraged the spread of disease. Frequent epidemics of typhoid and cholera claimed many lives. In 1861, Queen Victoria's husband, Prince Albert, died from typhoid. This tragic event highlighted the problems of public health in towns and encouraged the government to take action. Laws were passed that gradually brought improvements to living conditions in the towns. Overcrowding was reduced and improvements were made to water supplies, sewage systems and rubbish collection.

Prince Albert, whose death led to improved living conditions.

This cartoon shows Death pouring out water from a polluted pump.

✤ Why do you think this cartoon was published?

DETECTIVE WORK

You can find out more about conditions in Victorian towns by looking in libraries and by searching the Internet. This site is particularly useful: www.spartacus.schoolnet.co.uk/Britain

HOW DID FACTORIES CHANGE THE WAY PEOPLE WORKED?

'When my father introduced machinery into his mill, the hours of labour were increased to twelve, for five days in the week, and eleven on Saturdays, making seventy-one hours in the week. Other mill owners worked their hands as much as eighty-four hours a week.'

Factory owner describing the hours in an early Victorian factory.

The introduction of factories completely changed many Victorians' lives. Before their invention, most people worked to fit in with the seasons. They got up at dawn and worked until dark, working longer in the summer than in the winter. They took breaks when they needed to, and chatted and sang to help pass the time.

However, because it was not very profitable to run machines in this irregular way, factory owners introduced a shift system based on a strict timetable. All the workers on a shift had to start and finish work at the same time every day, whatever the season. Some workers worked at night and slept during the day. For the first time in history, ordinary people began to run their lives by the clock.

These workers are going home after a long, hard day at a factory.

Working in a Victorian factory was boring, repetitive and exhausting. While craftsmen had the satisfaction of making things from start to finish, factory workers saw only a small part of what was being made. They could no longer work at their own pace but had to keep up with the machines.

It was common for people in factories to work for fifteen hours a day with only fifteen minutes each for breakfast and tea, and half an hour for lunch.

Factory workers had to obey very strict rules. Money could be deducted from their wages for many things including turning up late, wasting materials and even whistling! The workers were supervised by overseers who bullied and beat people to make sure that they obeyed the rules and worked hard at all times.

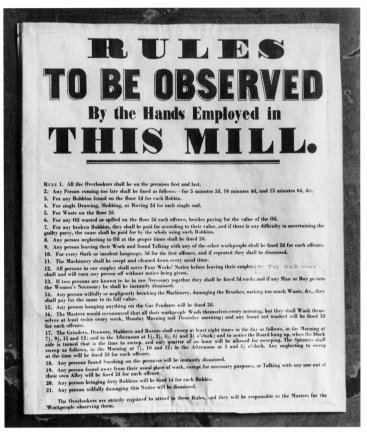

Mill workers in Salford had to obey these strict rules.

DETECTIVE WORK

Many factory workers gave evidence to the government officials who investigated how factories were run. Copies of these reports can be found on the websites listed on page 31.

Factory children would often be beaten to keep them awake.

How did Victorian children feel after working fifteen hours in a factory?

How safe were Victorian factories?

Victorian factories were often unpleasant and hazardous places to work. At first, there were no laws to make factory owners responsible for the health and safety of their workers. Accidents were frequent and often fatal.

Factory owners lost money if their machines were stopped. This child has been forced to clean under a loom while it is still running.

Machinery was dangerous to use and it was easy for people to be dragged into the mechanism by loose hair and clothing. Most at risk were those children who were employed to clean dirt from under machines that were still running. In 1844, a law was introduced to force factory owners to put guards on some machines, but it took much longer for the law to be obeyed.

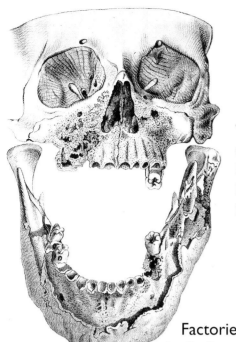

This worker's skull has been badly damaged by phosphorus in a factory.

DETECTIVE WORK

Charles Dickens visited factories to research his writing, but also used evidence from government reports. The Encyclopedia of British History website contains extracts from government reports on factory conditions. You can find its address on page 31.

Factories were usually badly lit, poorly aired and unbearably hot. People worked for hours amid the deafening roar of machinery and breathed an atmosphere that was thick with dust, steam and fumes. Some workers had to use dangerous chemicals that could permanently damage their health. People who used a poisonous substance called phosphorus to make matches lost their teeth as the chemicals ate away at the bones in their jaws.

If people were injured or became ill because of working in factories, they were not entitled to any compensation or help from the government. Workers who were off work through illness received no pay. If they were no longer able to work at all, then they would have to hope that their family could support them. If this was not possible, then they would end up begging on the streets or living in the workhouse. Poor people dreaded being sent to workhouses because they were like prisons.

Charles Dickens wrote about factory life in his novel *Hard Times* (1854).

'Cotton spinners work in a heat of 80–84°F [27–29°C]. They are locked in, except for half an hour at tea-time. They cannot send for water to drink, despite the heat. Then there is the dust and fuzz, which they breathe in. Men are aged by it; they cannot work after fifty years of age. Children are deformed and made ill.'

William Cobbett – Victorian reformer

WHY DID FACTORY OWNERS EMPLOY WOMEN AND CHILDREN?

Women generally earned half as much as men to do the same jobs, and children earned even less. So, it was much cheaper for factory owners to employ them.

Some factories employed orphans as apprentices. These children received no payment for their work other than food and a place to sleep. In most cases, the food was bad and the beds dirty. Apprentices had no one to protect them, so they were given the worst jobs in the factory and received the harshest treatment from the overseers.

Sometimes, apprentices ran away to escape the hard life in the factories. If they were caught and brought back they could expect to be beaten and locked up in rooms with no light and only a blanket to sleep on. Girls sometimes had their hair cut off to set an example to the other apprentices.

Women working in a pen factory, 1851.

✿ The women in the picture above are making nibs for pens. Why do you think that women were selected to do this job?

These young workers are queuing for their wages. Some are too poor to afford shoes.

The women in this Wigan factory are fortunate enough to have a lunch hour – in many factories this was not the case.

Eventually, laws were introduced to offer some protection to women and children working in factories. In 1850, for example, a law was passed limiting their working day to ten hours. Laws were also passed to ensure that factory apprentices received better treatment and a basic education.

As conditions improved, some women began to enjoy the independence and friendships that came with working in factories. Women's wages became an essential part of the family income in many parts of the country. In these areas, new businesses such as fish and chip shops were set up to cater for women who no longer had time for cooking at home.

'My girls work, I can find none. When the mills are busy they work from three in the morning 'til ten or half past ten at night. They are so tired at the end of the working day that they have to be beaten to keep them awake. When they get home they are so tired that they fall asleep with their supper still in their mouths.'

Father of two girls working in a cotton mill

DETECTIVE WORK

How does your school day compare to that of a child working in a Victorian factory? You will be able to find lots of evidence on Victorian child workers on the Internet.

How did life improve for factory workers?

In the early part of Queen Victoria's reign, most well-off people seemed unconcerned with the harsh lives that the poor factory workers had to endure. However, this gradually changed as reformers drew attention to conditions in the factories and towns, and persuaded people of the need for improvements.

Many reformers, such as the Earl of Shaftesbury, believed that it was their Christian duty to help those less fortunate than themselves. Shaftesbury wrote reports on the factories and mines that persuaded politicians to pass laws protecting the women and children who worked in them.

At first, such laws had little effect because many employers simply ignored them or found ways of bending the rules. Factory inspectors were appointed to enforce the new regulations. To start with there were not enough inspectors to make much of an impact, but as their numbers grew the bosses were forced to take them seriously.

The Earl of Shaftesbury wanted to improve conditions for Victorian workers.

A factory inspector taking evidence from child workers.

✖ The man watching the factory inspection is probably an overseer. Do you think his presence would affect what the children tell the inspector?

A cartoon by Robert Cruikshank draws attention to the plight of factory children.

DETECTIVE WORK

Look for biographies of reformers such as Dickens, Chadwick and Shaftesbury. These can be found in libraries or on the Internet.

Sir Edwin Chadwick.

Another reformer was Sir Edwin Chadwick. He wrote a best-selling book called *The Report on the Sanitary Condition of the Labouring Classes*. This painted a shocking picture of life in the poor parts of towns and led to new laws being passed. Councils were now forced to clean up the streets and provide proper sewers and water supplies.

Newspaper editors and journalists added their voices to the reforming campaigns. Writers such as Charles Dickens used popular novels to persuade both the public and politicians of the need for improvements. Such efforts eventually paid off and conditions in the factories and towns gradually improved. Life was generally much more comfortable for factory workers at the end of Victoria's reign than it had been at the beginning.

'It was a town of machinery and tall chimneys… It had a black canal in it, and a river that ran purple with ill-smelling dye, and vast piles of buildings full of windows where there was a rattling and a trembling all day long, and where the piston of the steam engine worked monotonously up and down…'

An extract from *Hard Times* (1854) by Charles Dickens – highlighting the bad conditions in a Victorian factory town.

How did factory workers protest?

The spread of factories meant that large numbers of people all worked in the same place. This made it much easier for them to join together to fight for better pay and working conditions. They did this by forming organizations called trade unions. There were many different types of union, each representing people who worked in a particular type of manufacturing or at a particular trade.

One of the main tactics used by unions to get what they wanted was by striking. When a strike was called, everyone who belonged to the union would refuse to turn up for work. They would gather at the factory gates in large crowds, or 'pickets', to persuade those who were not members of the union to stay away as well.

DETECTIVE WORK

Were there any strikes in your area during Victorian times? You may find library books on the history of local unions. Local trade union offices may also be able to help.

Police breaking up a demonstration by match workers in 1871.

✿ This Victorian illustration shows the police attacking women and children with truncheons. What do you think the illustrator was trying to say?

A march by match workers to protest against their working conditions and their treatment by the police.

Factories were particularly vulnerable to strikes. To make a profit, factory owners relied on all of their workers being in the right place at the right time. However, determined employers would hire other workers to beat the strike. The police or soldiers would be called in to break up the pickets. This often led to violent battles with many injuries on both sides.

At first, the government and employers refused to accept the fact that unions represented the workers. Strikes and pickets were illegal and could result in workers losing their jobs. As the public became more sympathetic to the plight of workers, the government passed laws giving them the right to strike. Bosses also came to accept that it was better to talk with the unions than to provoke costly strikes.

'The objects of trade unions are in general of a twofold character –

First: those of an ordinary friendly or benefit society – to afford relief to members of the union incapacitated from work [unable to work] by accident or sickness; to allow a sum for the funeral expenses of members and their wives.

Secondly: those of a trade society proper – to watch over and promote the interests of the working classes – and especially to protect them against undue advantage which the command of a large capital is supposed by them to give to the employers of labour.'

An extract from the Royal Commission Report on Trade Unions

WHAT WAS A FRIENDLY SOCIETY?

In the nineteenth century, people received very little help from the government if they fell on hard times. Ordinary working people had to find other ways of joining together to improve their lives and protect themselves from unexpected misfortunes. Many of the better-paid workers joined friendly societies. These offered insurance against illness and unemployment in return for regular weekly payments.

Much of the factory workers' wages was spent on food and other essentials – these were often expensive and of poor quality. In 1844, a group of weavers in Rochdale decided to open their own shop selling quality goods at a fair price. Customers could become members of the co-operative that ran the shop, and received a share of the profits. The idea was a great success and soon there were Co-op shops all over the country. Customers can still apply to become members of modern Co-op shops, which operate on the same principles as those in Victorian times.

✿ What sort of goods could people buy from the shop shown below?

A photo of a Co-op store in Woolwich, London, taken around the end of Victoria's reign.

DETECTIVE WORK

Was there a Co-op shop in your area in Victorian times? To find out, look in the local history section of your nearest big library or write to your local Co-op head office.

An open-air Chartist meeting, held on Kennington Common, London in 1848.

'Government was designed to protect the freedom and promote the happiness of… the whole people… Any form of government which fails (to do this)… is tyrannical, and ought to be amended or resisted.'

Extract from a Chartist proclamation

Many working people wanted the government to do more to help them. However, in 1837, only wealthy men could vote in elections or sit in Parliament. This meant that laws tended to favour the rich. Groups known as Chartists organized petitions and demonstrations across the country demanding that all men be allowed to vote.

An election poster supporting Keir Hardie.

The Chartists attracted a good deal of support from working people, but it was not until 1867 that all men gained the right to vote. This change in the voting system eventually led to the election of Keir Hardie, the first socialist MP (member of parliament), in 1892. The Independent Labour Party was formed in 1893. Although slow in coming, such political developments helped to persuade governments to pay more attention to the problems of poor working people.

VOTE FOR

Home Rule.

Democratic Government.

Justice to Labour

No Monopoly.

No Landlordism

Temperance Reform.

Healthy Homes.

Fair Rents.

Eight-Hour Day.

Work for the Unemployed.

KEIR HARDIE.

Printed and Published by F. W. Sear sr & Co, [L.S.C], 151, Barking Road, Canning Town, London, E.

WERE ALL BOSSES BAD?

Robert Owen (left) owned cotton mills in New Lanark (above).

Factory owners became richer and more powerful during Victorian times. Some made fortunes and lived like country gentlemen on huge estates built far away from the pollution and noise of the factory towns.

Many bosses were only interested in profit, and cared little for the welfare of their employees. However, some bosses adopted a more caring approach. Among these was Robert Owen, a mill owner from New Lanark in Scotland. Owen paid good wages and reduced the working hours of his employees. He also provided them with well-built houses, ran a school for the children and refused to employ anybody under ten years of age.

✿ Using this picture on the left as evidence, would you say that the painter wanted to show Robert Owen as a good or bad boss?

Owen was not the only factory owner to act in this way. In 1853, Titus Salt moved his workers away from the dirt and pollution of Bradford to 'Saltaire', a light and airy factory surrounded by 850 comfortable new homes. In 1888, soap maker William Lever built a similar scheme at Port Sunlight on Merseyside. George Cadbury followed suit in 1893 by building the 'model village' of Bournville for workers at his Birmingham chocolate factory.

While these employers seemed to have the interests of their workers at heart, they also realized that people worked better if they were happy and healthy. Other bosses slowly came to see the sense in this approach and began to behave in a more caring manner. By the end of Victoria's reign, social events and works outings had become a regular feature of factory life, as bosses sought to use perks instead of punishments to get the most out of their workers.

'It does not appear to me necessary for children to be employed under ten years of age in any regular work. I instruct them and give them exercise.'

Robert Owen

DETECTIVE WORK

Look for biographies of Robert Owen in the library or on the Internet. Learning about his life may help you to understand why he treated his workers better than other bosses.

These Victorians are enjoying a works outing to the seaside.

WHERE DID VICTORIANS GO SHOPPING?

DETECTIVE WORK
Many museums have examples of the factory-made goods that Victorians bought and used in their homes. Some will also have displays of advertising and packaging. Search The 24-Hour Museum website to find out which museum you could visit (see page 31).

During Victorian times the development of factories enabled Britain to become one of the wealthiest countries in the world. British factories imported large amounts of raw materials and exported finished goods all over the globe. In Britain, the shops were filled with new and exciting things to buy.

Department stores like Jenner's in Edinburgh became very popular in Victorian times.

'Shop till you drop could have been coined in the nineteenth century when it seemed that anything could be bought… Food, fashion and furnishings, books, toys and beauty preparations – the Victorian shopper wanted them all.'

Modern Historian,
Maurice Barren – 1998.

In some parts of the country working people were moved from slums to new estates with wide streets, improved water supplies and better sewage systems.

Most Victorians' lives improved during the nineteenth century. Wages rose and factory production lowered prices so that people could afford to buy more things. Changes in the way people worked had created a middle class whose homes were filled with labour-saving gadgets and luxury goods. The homes of working people, although they were never luxurious, also became more comfortable.

Shopping became an increasingly popular pastime. In towns and cities, big department stores were built offering a wide range of goods for sale under one roof. Elegant iron-and-glass arcades sprang up offering Victorians a more comfortable indoor shopping experience. These covered streets were the forerunners of today's American 'precincts' and shopping malls.

With so many new products in the shops, companies had to work harder to sell their goods. Advertising developed as manufacturers tried to persuade people to buy their brands rather than those of rival firms. Victorian towns and cities were plastered with posters promoting things as varied as hair oil and safety bicycles. Packaging design became more elaborate and colourful to help different products to stand out on shop shelves.

A bright and gaudy Victorian advertisement for oil heaters.

What was the Great Exhibition?

Crowds marvelled at the displays in the Great Exhibition.

In 1851, the Great Exhibition was held in London's Hyde Park. The idea for the event came from a man called Henry Cole, but a large part of its success was due to its promotion by Queen Victoria's husband, Prince Albert.

The aim of the exhibition was to provide a showcase for British manufacturing and to win new orders from abroad. The exhibition was held in a huge iron-and-glass building called the Crystal Palace. This was designed by Joseph Paxton and was a remarkable feat of engineering. Although it was 600 metres long and 120 metres wide, and contained 300,000 panes of glass, the building was completed in just fifteen months. This was possible because Paxton used factory techniques to mass-produce parts that could be quickly assembled on site.

Detective work

Find out more information about the Great Exhibition in the library or on the Internet.

The Crystal Palace was built especially for the Great Exhibition.

'...went to the machinery part where we stayed for two hours. What used to be done by hand and used to take months is now done in a few instants by the most beautiful machinery.'

Queen Victoria at the Great Exhibition.

For many wealthy visitors, the Great Exhibition provided a unique opportunity to see factory machinery at work.

The exhibition was so popular that it was attended by over 6 million people in just twenty weeks. People travelled from all over the country and special excursions were organized by railway and omnibus companies. The crowds that trooped through the exhibition halls would have seen an amazing assortment of manufactured goods from Britain and the rest of the world. These ranged in size from steam engines and factory machinery to delicate ornaments and toys. There were gadgets galore, including a pocket knife with eighty blades and a bed that could tip people into a cold bath to wake them up!

Many people saw the exhibition as proof that Britain was the world's leading industrial nation. Although Britain soon lost this advantage to countries such as Germany and the USA, the role that Victorian Britain played in the development of factories had more lasting effects. The advances and changes that were caused by industrialization played a large part in shaping how life would be lived in the future.

❀ Read the quote on this page. Do you think that factory workers would have described the machinery they used as beautiful?

YOUR PROJECT

If you have been following the detective work at the end of each section, you should have found plenty of clues. These clues will help you to create your own project about Victorian factories.

First, you will need to choose a topic that interests you. You could use one of the questions below as a starting point.

Topic Questions
- What was life like for Victorian factory workers?
- How did the development of factories affect your area in Victorian times?
- How did improvements in the manufacture of goods affect people's lives?
- Why was Victorian Britain called the 'workshop of the world'?
- How did the lives of factory workers improve during the Victorian period?
- Were all factory bosses bad?

Factory workers usually lived in very basic conditions.

When you have gathered all your information, think of an interesting way to present it. You might like to use one of the ideas below.

The factory workers above are making shoes.

Project Presentation
● Write your project in the form of a Victorian worker's diary.
● Present your project in the style of a Victorian newspaper.
● Make a poster for a Victorian manufacturing company, showing how the things being produced in factories improved people's lives.
● Write a pamphlet or newspaper article protesting at the living and working conditions suffered by Victorian factory workers.

These young people made and sold matches.

You might find an unusual subject for your topic. Sherlock Bones found out that some leading Victorians were very much in favour of children working in factories. You could present your topic as a debate between these people and the reformers. You can find out more about the views of both sides on the Encyclopedia of British History website (see page 31).

GLOSSARY

apprentice A young person who is trained to do a job and forced by law to work at that job for a fixed length of time.

cholera An often fatal disease caught through infected water supplies.

compensation Money or goods given to make up for injury or death at work.

discipline Rules that have to be obeyed.

export To send things out of one country to another.

'flying shuttle' A machine for weaving fabric, invented in Victorian times.

friendly society A club that looks after its members in times of sickness, unemployment or death.

hand loom A machine that weaved yarn into fabric. It was powered by hand.

import To bring things into one country from another.

Industrial Revolution A phrase used by historians to describe the changes which turned Britain from a rural, agricultural country into an urban, industrial one.

manufacture Make things by hand or machine, usually on a large scale.

overseer A person who makes sure that workers do their jobs properly.

pickets Workers who demonstrate outside a place of work during a strike to persuade others not to work.

reform Make changes for the better.

'spinning jenny' A machine for spinning yarn, invented in Victorian times.

spinning wheel An old-fashioned machine for spinning yarn.

strike Workers agreeing together not to work until their employer meets their demands.

textile Cloth (e.g. wool or cotton).

trade union An organization for people in the same kind of work, which looks after their pay, hours and safety.

typhoid A severe infection.

yarn Thread that is used for weaving or knitting.

ANSWERS

page 7
✿ The rioters are going to use axes and burning torches to destroy the factory and its machinery.

page 9
✿ The cartoon was published to persuade people of the need to provide clean water supplies to prevent the spread of fatal diseases.

page 11
✿ After a long, hard day at the factory, Victorian children would be exhausted and probably just want to sleep.

page 14
✿ As well as being cheaper to employ than men, women were thought to be better suited to delicate work because they had smaller and nimbler fingers.

page 16
✿ The children would probably be too afraid to say bad things about the factory where they worked if their overseer was watching them. It was quite common at first for overseers to be present during a factory inspector's visit.

page 18
✿ By showing the police beating women and children the illustrator was trying to persuade people to support the demonstrators. The illustrator emphasized the point by adding the following ironic caption: 'Gallant conduct by the police – heroic attack upon the little match makers and match sellers'.

page 20
✿ The shop sign tells us that the shop was selling a range of goods including meat, groceries, clothing and fabrics.

page 22

🐾 The artist who drew this portrait of Robert Owen may have tried to create the impression that he was important but kind. This view of Robert Owen is supported by what we know of how he treated his factory employees.

page 27

🐾 People who had to work long hours on factory machinery may not have found them as beautiful as Queen Victoria did.

Books to read

Victorian Shopping by Maurice Baren (Michael O'Mara Books, 2000).

The Victorians: Reconstructed by Liz Gogerly (Hodder Wayland, 2003).

Life & Work in 19th Century Britain by R Hamer (Heinemann, 1995).

Victorian Factories by Andrew Langley (Heinemann, 1996).

Victorian Factory by Marilyn Tolhurst (A & C Black, 1996).

Useful websites

The 24-Hour Museum
www.24hourmuseum.org.uk

Encyclopedia of British History
www.spartacus.schoolnet.co.uk

History World
www.historyworld.net

National Archives
http://learningcurve.pro.gov.uk/bbc

School History
www.schoolhistory.co.uk

Robert Owen Museum
http://robert-owen.midwales.com

Places to visit

Blists Hill Open Air Museum, Telford, Shropshire.

Bradford Industrial & Horses at Work Museum, Yorkshire.

Coalisland Corn Mill, County Tyrone.

Derby Industrial Museum, Derby.

Leeds Industrial Museum.

Long Shop Museum, Leiston, Suffolk.

Maritime & Industrial Museum, Swansea.

Merseyside Museum of Labour History, Liverpool.

New Lanark Visitor Centre, Lanark.

North of England Open-air Museum, Beamish, Tyne & Wear.

Port Sunlight Heritage Centre, Merseyside.

Quarry Bank Mill, Styal, Cheshire.

Robert Owen Museum, Newtown, Powys.

INDEX